THE LOTHIANS' LAST DAYS OF S

by
W.A.C. Smith

Class J36 0-6-0 No. 65234, a former North British Railway locomotive built in 1891, is seen upon arrival at Haddington on 29 August 1964 with a Stephenson Locomotive Society railtour, having successfully surmounted the 2-mile climb at 1 in 66 out of Longniddry. The county town of Haddington had hoped to have its station on the main line, but instead became the terminus of a 4¾-mile branch. It suffered a further indignity in 1949 when its passenger service was one of the first in Scotland to be withdrawn by the recently formed Scottish Region of British Railways (freight traffic continued until 1968), while a proposed preservation scheme for the branch by the Scottish Railway Preservation Society has, instead, come to fruition at Bo'ness.

ISBN 1 84033 353 7

The publishers regret that they cannot supply copies of any pictures featured in this book.

Photographed on 20 August 1960, class V3 2-6-2T No. 67666 pauses at Drem, junction station for the North Berwick branch, with the 4.12 p.m. train from Dunbar to Edinburgh Waverley.

INTRODUCTION

Wednesday, 19 June 1946, was a fine, sunny day when, having purchased third class return tickets at a cost of seven shillings, I made my way along platform two at Glasgow's Queen Street Station to join the 11.20 a.m. train for Edinburgh Waverley. This comprised class A4 Pacific No. 4488, 'Union of South Africa', still in wartime black livery, at the head of ten coaches.

The object of my visit was a two-day exhibition of locomotives and rolling stock being held at Waverley Station to celebrate the centenary of the opening of the North British Railway from Edinburgh to Berwick – the first railway across the border – on 18 June 1846. The exhibition occupied platforms five and six at the east end of the station and featured class A4 Pacific No. 14, ' Silver Link', A1 Pacific No. 4470, 'Great Northern', A2 Pacific (rebuilt 2-8-2) No. 2001, 'Cock o' the North', B1 4-6-0 No. 1048, L1 2-6-4T No. 9000, diesel shunter No. 8000 and preserved Great Northern Railway 4-2-2 No. 1. Also on show were examples of new coaching stock, a 45-ton breakdown crane, a Mobile Signalling School and a North British Railway horsedrawn 'dandy coach.'

My return journey from Waverley was by the 6.10 p.m. train – nine corridor coaches and a brake van – taken over upon its arrival from London Kings Cross by class D11 4-4-0 No. 6395, 'Ellen Douglas', and, as on the outward journey, was run to time throughout.

Having 'copped' my first Hunt class 4-4-0, No. 377 'The Tynedale', when passing Glasgow's Eastfield shed, followed by Sentinel steam railcar 'Royal Eagle' at Waverley, together with Q6 0-8-0 No. 3364 and D34 4-4-0 No. 9221 'Glen Orchy' (this Glen was the last of the class I needed for marking off in my Ian Allan ABC of LNER locomotives), it seemed that the glory days had returned after years of wartime austerity which were summed up by the slogan, 'Is your journey really necessary?' However, within eighteen months the dead hand of nationalisation was to fall on Britain's railways.

As early as the seventeenth century, there were primitive waggonways serving coal pits in the Lothians. However, in 1831 the Edinburgh & Dalkeith Railway was opened and, although horse-operated and of a non-standard 4 ft 6 in. gauge, was of double track and carried not only coal to the capital, but also passengers. It was extended to Leith in 1838 and was acquired by the North British Railway in 1845.

Following upon opening of the Edinburgh & Glasgow Railway in 1842, the North British Railway had been promoted to build a line from Edinburgh southwards to Dunbar and Berwick. Opened in 1846, this now forms part of the East Coast main line. The West Coast main line was created in 1848 with the opening of the Caledonian Railway from Carlisle, dividing at Carstairs for Glasgow and Edinburgh.

The next fifty years saw a substantial expansion of the railway network, with routes pushing out from Edinburgh to Lothians and Border towns and local lines penetrating the coalfields and mill valleys. There were rivalries at Leith and Granton for dock traffic, while in 1868 a line reached South Queensferry in anticipation of a bridge across the Firth of Forth. This, however, did not materialise until 1890, construction having been delayed by the fall of the first Tay Bridge in 1879.

The coming of the twentieth century brought a virtual end to railway construction, one of the last projects being the Lothian Lines (opened by the North British Railway in 1915), intended to facilitate the shipment of coal through the port of Leith and, as first planned, a throwback to the early days of railways with colliery owners providing their own motive power and wagons.

The Railway Grouping of 1923 resulted in the North British Railway forming part of the London & North Eastern Railway (LNER) and the Caledonian Railway going to the London, Midland & Scottish Railway (LMS).

Despite minor line closures, the 1930s brought a short-lived railway renaissance. Once seen, who could forget the sight of the streamlined express, 'The Coronation', in two-tone garter blue livery and hauled by one of the LNER's magnificent class A4 Pacifics, streaking across the cornfields of East Lothian.

Soon after the formation of British Railways in 1948 the elimination of its 20,000 steam locomotives became an end in itself, under the false premise that this would solve BR's spiralling financial problems which – in fact – were to worsen, despite a (botched) modernisation programme followed by the Beeching cuts in service.

Steam working ended within the Scottish Region of British Railways on 1 May 1967, although London Midland Region locomotives continued to appear north of the border until the end of that year. Steam was eliminated from British Railways in August 1968.

Photographed on 1 May 1954, class C16 former North British Railway 4-4-2T No. 67495 is seen upon arrival at North Berwick with the 4.31 p.m. from Drem.

Class V1 2-6-2T No. 67659 awaits departure from North Berwick with the 6.13 p.m. to Edinburgh Waverley on 1 May 1954. The 4¾-mile branch, opened in 1850, survived several threats of closure to be electrified along with the East Coast main line in 1991, but with its terminus reduced to an uncovered single platform.

East Fortune was not an original station on the North British main line, but had been opened by 1850. The only occasion on which I used it was on 20 August 1960 when I joined the 5.38 p.m. train from Edinburgh to Dunbar hauled by class D49 4-4-0 No. 62711, 'Dumbartonshire'. The name carried by this locomotive, built at Darlington in 1928, perpetuated a common mistake as the correct name for the county is Dunbartonshire. 'Morayshire' of this class is preserved as LNER No. 246 at Bo'ness.

Opposite: Class A4 Pacific No. 60023, 'Golden Eagle', passes East Fortune with the 9.15 a.m. express from York to Glasgow Queen Street on 24 August 1963. The station was closed the following year upon withdrawal of the local service between Edinburgh and Berwick. East Fortune is probably best known for its First World War airfield, from which the airship R34 set off in 1919 to make the first return crossing by air of the Atlantic, and where a Concorde supersonic airliner is now housed within the Museum of Flight.

The station at East Linton, originally without the prefix and 2½ miles from East Fortune, served the public from 1846 until 1964. On 24 August 1963 I photographed class V2 2-6-2 No. 60858 hurrying through with the 8.45 a.m. from Leeds to Glasgow Queen Street.

On 20 August 1960 class D49 4-4-0 No. 62718, 'Kinross-shire', worked the 6.50 p.m. train from Dunbar to Edinburgh and I photographed it arriving at East Linton's attractive station before getting aboard. This particular train omitted calls at several intermediate stations and the "Shire", of a class of locomotive not normally noted for fast running, gave a high speed run on this occasion. Perhaps the crew had plans for a Saturday night out!

On 24 August 1963 class B1 4-6-0 No. 61219 was photographed passing West Barns siding as it approached Dunbar with the 5.38 p.m. from Edinburgh Waverley.

Standard 2-6-4T No. 80114 runs into Dunbar on 8 September 1962 with the 5.38 p.m. from Edinburgh Waverley. Dunbar Station, nowadays reduced to a single platform, is situated on a sharp curve and when fast tracks, seen on the left, became necessary they bypassed it on an easier alignment ('fast tracks' refers to a less severe curvature to allow higher speeds by non-stop trains).

Standard tank No. 80054 at Dunbar shed on 8 September 1962, prior to working the 6.50 p.m. semi-fast service to Edinburgh. The shed, the only occupant of which on this occasion was class B1 4-6-0 No. 61354, was closed in 1964 and demolished.

The small town of Musselburgh, situated at the mouth of the River Esk, had its first station on the North British main line of 1846, but this station was renamed Inveresk upon the opening in 1847 of a branch from Newhailes to Musselburgh, taking in part of the early Edinburgh & Dalkeith Railway. On 21 May 1955 driver J. Wood of St Margaret's depot posed at the terminus with class V1 2-6-2T No. 67668, heading the 6.29 p.m. departure for Edinburgh Waverley. Newhailes Station had been closed in 1950, and the branch lost its passenger service in 1964, but freight traffic continued until 1970. In 1988 a new Musselburgh Station, served by North Berwick trains, was opened on the main line.

Inveresk (originally Musselburgh) is seen here on 28 April 1962 with class V3 2-6-2T No. 67649 arriving with the 3.45 p.m. from Dunbar to Edinburgh. The station was closed in 1964.

Former Smeaton Station seen on the occasion of a Railway Society of Scotland railtour on 27 August 1966, with class J36 0-6-0 No. 65345 rounding the train. Smeaton, situated south of Monktonhall Junction on the East Coast main line, served several collieries and was junction for an odd collection of lines – to Ormiston, Macmerry and Gifford – which were constructed comparatively late in the Railway Age and which closed for passengers as early as the 1920s and 30s.

Dalkeith Station was at the end of a ½-mile branch opened in 1839 from the horse-worked Edinburgh & Dalkeith Railway 'main line', which ran from the city at St Leonards to Dalhousie. The LNER ended the passenger service from Waverley in 1942 as a wartime economy measure. On 24 May 1962 I travelled on the footplate of the last active class J35 0-6-0, No. 64510, which was working the afternoon 'conditional' (ie. it only ran if required) freight trip to Hardengreen Yard at Eskbank and I photographed it preparing to propel the train from Dalkeith to Glenesk Junction, where reversal was necessary. In 1964 freight facilities were withdrawn from Dalkeith.

Also on 24 May 1962 I travelled from Polton with No. 64510 which was hauling three vans from the local paper mill. These can be seen in the photograph being shunted at the small terminus deep in the valley of the North Esk. Opened in 1867, its passenger service had ended in 1951. Polton was the smallest of what were known as the Southern branches – the others being to Glencorse, Penicuik and Peebles – opened between 1855 and 1877 and all now closed.

The Glencorse branch served collieries at Loanhead, Bilston Glen and Roslin. The passenger service was withdrawn as long ago as 1933, but mineral traffic lingered on until the early 1990s. On 21 October 1963 class J37 0-6-0 No. 64624 was photographed passing Ramsay Colliery at Loanhead with a loaded coal train.

Although dieselised in 1958, the Peebles line was closed to all traffic four years later. Being at that time Scottish Area Secretary for the Stephenson Locomotive Society, I organised a 'Farewell to Peebles' train for the last day of services (3 February 1962), hauled by class J37 0-6-0 No. 64587. The journey included a call at Rosslynlee Hospital Halt which had been opened as recently as 1958. The special, seen here, was probably the only steam train to have called there.

The North British line from Portobello to Hawick utilised part of the former Edinburgh & Dalkeith Railway and was opened throughout in 1849, being extended to Carlisle in 1862 to form the Waverley Route which was closed in 1969. Engineering works included the 22-arch Newbattle Viaduct, spanning the River South Esk near Newtongrange, where class B1 4-6-0 No. 61341 was photographed on 24 May 1962, hauling the 5.11 p.m. from Edinburgh Waverley to Galashiels.

The Lady Victoria Colliery at Newtongrange was sunk by the Lothian Coal Co. in 1890, being described in contemporary press reports as a 'revolutionary pit'. It made Newtongrange the largest mining village in Scotland. By the late 1960s it was part of the Scottish South Area of the National Coal Board and had an interesting collection of pugs including 0-4-2T No. 7, built in 1914 by Grant, Ritchie & Co. of Kilmarnock. I photographed it in action on 16 February 1971. Rail traffic ceased early the following year.

In evening sunshine standard 2-6-4T No. 80055 nears Gorebridge with the 5.11 p.m. local train from Edinburgh Waverley on 11 May 1963. It seems likely that the Waverley Route will be reopened between Edinburgh and Galashiels, but as a single track only with all the possible problems of line capacity, speed restrictions and punctuality which this may entail.

Class 4MT 2-6-0 No. 76049 leaves Gorebridge on 26 September 1964 with the 12 noon train from Hawick to Edinburgh Waverley.

The Caledonian Railway was opened from Carlisle in 1848, forking at Carstairs for Glasgow and Edinburgh. Branches from the latter to Granton and Leith followed and then, in 1874, the Balerno branch was opened from the then outskirts of the city at Slateford along the wooded valley of the Water of Leith to rejoin the main line at Ravelrig Junction. In 1943 the passenger service was suspended, never to be resumed, although the line remained open for freight until the 1960s. During this period there were several special trains for enthusiasts and that of 20 June 1962 is seen here near Balerno, hauled by class 2P 0-4-4T No. 55260 of Caledonian design.

There was a station on the Balerno branch at Currie and, following its 'temporary' closure in 1943 (ultimately, it never reopened), alternative facilities were available at Curriehill Station on the main line until closure of that station in 1951. This photograph shows standard class 5 4-6-0 No. 73055 passing through the former Curriehill Station on 20 June 1964 with the 12.30 p.m. train from Glasgow Central to Edinburgh Princes Street. The station was reopened to commuters in 1987.

Midcalder Station on the Caley main line was opened as Kirknewton. On 5 July 1958, the last day of full steam working, Black Five No. 45030 was photographed with the 6.10 p.m. from Edinburgh Princes Street to Glasgow Central. The station has since reverted back to its original name.

Opening of the Cleland & Midcalder Railway in 1869 not only gave the Caledonian Railway access to an important coal mining and shale oil producing area, but shortened the mileage (previously via Carstairs) between Edinburgh and Glasgow. This enabled the company to compete with the North British Railway for the traffic and this continued into the LMS/LNER era until the outbreak of war in 1939. On 25 May 1963 well-cleaned former LNER class B1 4-6-0 No. 61261, complete with Caledonian route indicator on the bufferbeam, was photographed passing through West Calder Station, bound for Edinburgh Princes Street with the summer Saturdays 9.20 a.m. from Heads of Ayr Holiday Camp Station.

A Review of the Territorial Army on its Golden Jubilee was held by the Queen in Edinburgh on 5 July 1958. In connection with this there was a military special at 6.50 a.m. from Hamilton Central to Edinburgh Princes Street, worked by preserved Caledonian Railway 4-2-2 No. 123 which had been returned to service earlier in the year. The return working was at 6.35 p.m. and I photographed No. 123 passing West Calder with the special which consisted of three former LMS non-corridor coaches. During the so-called 'Race to Edinburgh' between the rival east and west coast railway companies in the 1880s, No. 123 had made a record run from Carlisle to Edinburgh. The Shotts line survived the Beeching cuts, but is reduced to an hourly service operated by outdated Sprinter units which call at all 20 stations and require a monumental one and a half hours for the 46½ miles. Yet, by electrifying the 23 miles between Holytown Junction and Midcalder Junction, a fast intercity route could be created.

The Edinburgh to Carstairs line was electrified in 1993 and has an 880 foot summit at Cobbinshaw, reached by a 6-mile climb from Midcalder Junction – much of it at a gradient of 1 in 100. On 5 October 1963 Coronation Pacific No. 46251, 'City of Nottingham', resplendent in maroon livery, made a magnificent spectacle as it topped the summit at speed with a railtour returning to Crewe from Edinburgh Princes Street. The only previous occasion that I had been on the ground at Cobbinshaw (rather than in a passing train) was during the great freeze of early 1947 when I was one of the squaddies from The Royal Scots shovelling several feet of snow to clear the tracks!

Photographed on 5 October 1963, three years before the closure of Cobbinshaw Station, Black Five No. 45185 passes through with a westbound freight train. Today, freight traffic – the very *raison d'etre* for our railways – is all but non-existent on them.

With the Forth Bridge in the background, class K4 2-6-0 No. 61998, 'Macleod of Macleod', rolls into Dalmeny Station on 11 June 1960 with a 7.10 p.m. relief train from Ladybank to Edinburgh Waverley, picking up homeward-bound Sunday school trips and the like from various small stations. The K4s were built for the West Highland Line by the LNER in 1937/38, but ended their days in Fife.

On 20 July 1959 former LMS Jubilee class 4-6-0 No. 45724, 'Warspite', allocated to Carlisle Kingmoor Motive Power Depot, was quite a way from its usual haunts when I photographed it approaching Dalmeny North Junction with the 3.36 p.m. train from Thornton Junction to Glasgow Queen Street.

Class A2 Pacific No. 60525, 'A.H. Peppercorn', passes Dalmeny North Junction on 20 July 1959 with the 4.17 p.m. from Edinburgh Waverley to Aberdeen. The connection to Winchburgh Junction on the Glasgow line goes off on the right while the South Queensferry branch drops away through the cutting on the left.

Class J36 0-6-0 No. 65258 was returning to Edinburgh as I photographed it climbing towards Dalmeny North Junction with the afternoon goods from South Queensferry on 15 August 1961. The branch, opened from Ratho on the Glasgow line in 1868, was extended to Port Edgar in 1878, but lost its passenger service in 1890 with the opening of the Forth Bridge approach lines with a new station at Dalmeny. South Queensferry was reopened for passengers in 1919, but closed again ten years later, with final closure coming in 1966 when the freight service ended.

Photographed on 26 December 1962, class J36 0-6-0 No. 65288 arrives at Queensferry Junction, Ratho, with the 'Ferry Goods' from Edinburgh and prepares to leave for South Queensferry, shunting as required at Kirkliston and Dalmeny naval stores depot *en route*. The sprinkling of snow and a biting wind were portents of the Arctic weather to come in early 1963.

Continuing west along the old Edinburgh & Glasgow Railway of 1842 (it was acquired by the North British in 1865) we reach Linlithgow. Now a busy commuter station, it was much quieter on 16 July 1960 when I photographed class B1 4-6-0 No. 61245, 'Murray of Elibank', arriving with the 4.28 p.m. from Crail to Glasgow Queen Street. The train included 'Silver Jubilee' stock from the pre-war streamlined express between London and Newcastle which had been carefully stored during the war. Unfortunately, British Railways did not see fit to restore luxury rail traffic and the coaches, with their armchair comfort, were scrapped soon after.

In 1851 the ancient port of Borrowstounness, now known as Bo'ness, was reached by an extension of the Slamannan Railway from Causewayend (on the Union Canal). This included a connecting curve to the Edinburgh & Glasgow main line at Manuel, but by then the port was already in decline following the opening of the Forth & Clyde Canal from neighbouring Grangemouth and this continued despite expansion of the dock by the North British Railway. The branch, nowadays home to the Scottish Railway Preservation Society, lost its passenger service in 1956 and on the last day, 5 May, I photographed class 4MT 2-6-0 No. 43141 passing along the foreshore, hauling the 1.57 p.m. from Bo'ness to Polmont.

Probably the last steam-hauled passenger train to use the former North British station at Bo'ness – today's preserved railway is on a new alignment – was the Branch Line Society's 'Scottish Central' railtour of 7 May 1960, consisting of former Caledonian Railway 4-4-0 No. 54465 with the two restored Caley coaches which are now preserved in the Scottish Railway Museum at Bo'ness. This ensemble was a not inappropriate choice for what had been a North British branch line as Caledonian trains had worked over it for a short time.

The only intermediate station on the Bo'ness branch was at Kinneil and this was closed in 1930. There was a colliery there, later forming part of the NCB Scottish North Area, where on 12 April 1971 I photographed four-coupled pug No. 21 which was built by Andrew Barclay & Co. of Kilmarnock in 1951 and formerly employed at Manor Powis Colliery, on the north side of the Forth, where it carried the number 17. Kinneil Colliery was closed in 1978.

The aforementioned Slamannan Railway became part of the Monklands Railways which were acquired by the North British Railway in 1865. The straggling, single track, mainly mineral railway originated at Coatbridge and divided at Blackston Junction for Bo'ness and Bathgate, passenger services and through freight workings being ended by the LNER in 1930. The Bathgate branch included a massive twelve-arch viaduct over the River Avon at Westfield Station where, on 19 June 1962, I photographed preserved North British Railway 4-4-0 No. 256, 'Glen Douglas', crossing with a railtour special. Our snow clearing efforts of March 1947 (see page 28) took in this branch and before leaving Bathgate a locomotive was attached on rear so that, in the event of our train becoming trapped in drifts, it could be drawn clear. Unfortunately – or, perhaps, fortunately – nothing as exciting as that was to happen!

A busy scene from the footbridge at the level crossing situated at the former Bathgate Lower Station, as class J36 0-6-0 No. 65290 propels empty wagons to Easton Colliery on 11 June 1963. The signal box prefers the old North British appellation of Lower Bathgate! The colliery remained in production until 1973.

Bathgate Upper Station was opened in 1849 upon arrival of the Edinburgh & Bathgate Railway. The Bathgate & Coatbridge Railway followed in 1862, and Glasgow was reached in 1870 to form a secondary route between the two cities. Passenger trains were slow and infrequent, but rich mineral fields were tapped. Bathgate Upper is seen here on 24 September 1955, with class D30 4-4-0 No. 62439, 'Father Ambrose', awaiting departure with the 11.47 a.m. to Glasgow Queen Street Low Level and terminating at Hyndland. Passenger services over the Bathgate line ended in 1956.

Bathgate Upper Station after closure. The date was 6 May 1961 and the occasion was the Branch Line Society 'Bathgate and District' railtour, which was worked by class N15 0-6-2T No. 69163. When a passenger service was restored between Edinburgh and Bathgate in the 1980s this was to a single platform situated a short distance to the east of the remains of the Upper station. However, there exists a possibility of restoring the line in its entirety.

The Bathgate line provided a useful diversionary route. On 6 July 1957 class B1 4-6-0 No. 61191 was photographed passing the East signal box on the approach to the Upper station with the summer Saturdays' 10.25 a.m. from Scarborough to Glasgow Queen Street Low Level.

Photographed on the evening of 6 May 1961, class J36 0-6-0 No. 65346 has banked a coal train, hauled by an equally venerable Caledonian 0-6-0, up to Armadale and awaits its next turn of duty in Bathgate East Yard. No. 65346, built by the North British Railway in 1900, was withdrawn from service in 1964. The motive power depot, seen on the left, was closed in 1966.

With line closures and rapidly increasing dieselisation, compounded by a marked decline in freight traffic following upon the 1955 ASLEF strike, numbers of steam locomotives being withdrawn from service exceeded scrapping capacity, resulting in dumps of condemned locomotives being established at several locations including Bathgate and Bo'ness. On 18 April 1959 there were eighteen redundant locos lined up at the Bathgate dump and this photograph shows class J88 0-6-0T No. 68339, class N15 0-6-2T No. 69162, and class Y9 0-4-0ST No. 68118 – all former North British railway shunting engines – awaiting their fate.

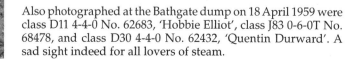

Also photographed at the Bathgate dump on 18 April 1959 were class D11 4-4-0 No. 62683, 'Hobbie Elliot', class J83 0-6-0T No. 68478, and class D30 4-4-0 No. 62432, 'Quentin Durward'. A sad sight indeed for all lovers of steam.

An Orange walk at Broxburn on 6 July 1957 resulted in the closed station at Uphall being temporarily reopened for four special trains from Airdrie and Coatbridge, each consisting of nine coaches. Black Five 4-6-0 No. 44902 is seen here passing through Bathgate Upper with the 5.10 p.m. return special for Airdrie.

At the west end of the former Bathgate Upper Station on 6 July 1957 class J36 0-6-0 No. 65344 waits to bank a mineral train for the 2½ miles up to Armadale, following J37 No. 64618 which was running some 25 minutes late with a 5.50 p.m. return Orange walk special from Uphall to Coatbridge Sunnyside. The line veering to the left in the foreground led to Bathgate Lower.

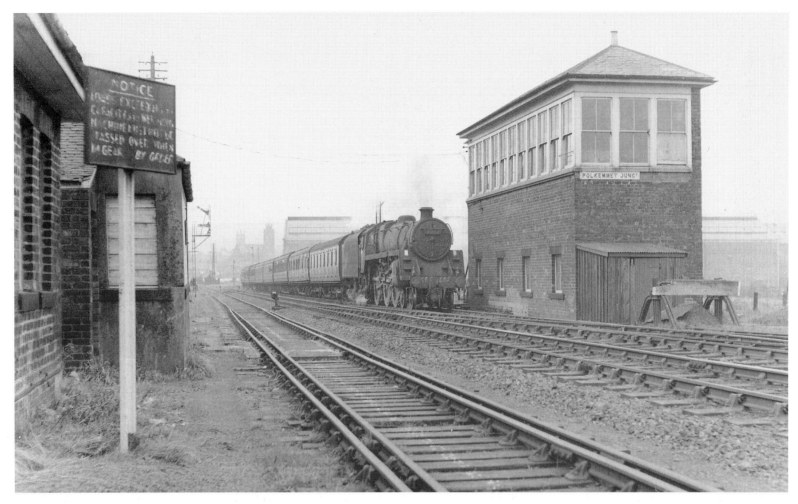

Following the electrification of Glasgow Queen Street Low Level Station in 1960, east-bound football specials used the city's St Enoch Station and joined the Airdrie line at High Street East Junction. On 22 September 1962 there were two such trains for Easter Road Park Halt at Edinburgh with return from Abbeyhill Station at 5.06 p.m. and 5.20 p.m. The first of the return trains, hauled by standard class 5 4-6-0 No. 73124 (from Corkerhill shed), is seen here passing Polkemmet Junction signal box which was situated a short distance to the west of Bathgate Upper Station and where the line to Bathgate Lower went off on the left and the old Wilsontown, Morningside & Coltness Railway diverged on the right.

In 1955 Bathgate Motive Power Depot had an allocation of 36 steam locomotives. Although mainly freight types and, with but one exception, all of North British Railway origin, two passenger engines were included, these being class D30 4-4-0 No. 62439, 'Father Ambrose', and class D34 4-4-0 No. 62495, 'Glen Luss'. However, on the last day of passenger services – 7 January 1956 – No. 62439 was not available for the 11.47 a.m. train to Hyndland and class J35 0-6-0 No. 64468 was substituted. It was duly photographed storming past Boghead Crossing on the climb from Bathgate to Armadale.

On a hot and sunny 11 June 1963 class J36 0-6-0 No. 65234, with a loaded coal train from Woodend Colliery, descends across somewhat featureless countryside to join the Bathgate line between Armadale and Westcraigs. The colliery closed in 1965.

WORLD IN PERIL

FORESTS
UNDER THREAT

PAUL MASON

Heinemann
LIBRARY

DUDLEY SCHOOLS LIBRARY SERVICE

www.heinemannlibrary.co.uk
Visit our website to find out more information about Heinemann Library books.

To order:
☎ Phone +44 (0) 1865 888066
🖨 Fax +44 (0) 1865 314091
💻 Visit www.heinemannlibrary.co.uk

Edited by Louise Galpine and Rachel Howells
Designed by Richard Parker and Manhattan Design
Picture research by Hannah Taylor and Rebecca Sodergren
Production by Alison Parsons
Originated by Dot Gradations Ltd.
Printed in China by Leo Paper Products Ltd.

ISBN 978 0 431020 58 7 (hardback)
13 12 11 10 09
10 9 8 7 6 5 4 3 2 1

British Library Cataloguing in Publication Data
Mason, Paul
Forests under threat. – (World in peril)
577.3

A full catalogue record for this book is available from the British Library.

Acknowledgements

We would like to thank the following for permission to reproduce photographs: Alamy pp. **8** (Lee Foster), **13** (Terry Whittaker), **27** (Steve Atkins Photography); Corbis pp. **7** (Martin Harvey), **9** (epa/ Martin Alipaz), **15** (John and Lisa Merrill); Corbis Sygma p. **23** (Yves Forestier); FLPA pp. **18** (Imagebroker/ ROM), **19** (Frans Lanting); FLPA/ Minden Pictures/ Mark Moffett p. **17** (FLPA); Getty Images p. **16** (Will and Deni McIntyre); Paul Mason p. **25**; Photolibrary pp. **6** (Nordic Photos), **11** (Corbis), **14** (Douglas Peebles), **20** (Lynn Stone), **24** (David Clapp); Reuters pp. **12** (Gregg Newton), **26** (Christophe Karaba); Science Photo Library p. **21** (Will and Deni McIntyre); SIME-4Corners Images p. **4** (Johannah Huber); Still Pictures pp. **10** (Hartmut Schwarzbach), **22** (Jeff Henry).

Cover photograph of cutting in tropical rainforest, Panama, reproduced with permission of Corbis (Frans Lanting).

We would like to thank Michael Mastrandrea for his invaluable help in the preparation of this book.

Every effort has been made to contact copyright holders of material reproduced in this book. Any omissions will be rectified in subsequent printings if notice is given to the publishers.

All the Internet addresses (URLs) given in this book were valid at the time of going to press. However, due to the dynamic nature of the Internet, some addresses may have changed, or sites may have changed or ceased to exist since publication. While the author and Publishers regret any inconvenience this may cause readers, no responsibility for any such changes can be accepted by either the author or the Publishers.

Contents

Some words are printed in bold, **like this**. You can find out what they mean by looking in the glossary.

What makes forests so important?

At one time, forests covered two-thirds of the land on Earth. Millions of different insects, plants, and animals lived among the trees. This great variety of living things is called **biodiversity**.

There are many different types of forest. In cold regions, huge forests of evergreen trees stretch so far that it takes days to travel through them. Further south, the trees grow more thinly, and **shed** their leaves in winter. Near the **equator**, the forests can be so thick that travellers have to cut plants down to clear their path.

Throughout history, forest plants and animals have been a source of food for people. Wood for building and heating has come from forests. Many medicines first came from forest plants.

Our planet's population is growing fast, and our demands on the forests are also increasing. Today, only 30 per cent of land is covered in forest. Half our forests have already been cut down – and the remaining forests are under threat.

How does this forest help the planet survive?

Imagine what it would be like to drift through the rainforest along this river. Like all forests, the rainforest is a crucial part of life on Earth. The trees take in the gas carbon dioxide, which helps them grow. They release oxygen, which humans and other animals need to survive. Because they breathe in carbon dioxide and breathe out oxygen, forests are sometimes called "the lungs of the planet".

Rainforest trees such as this one take years to grow, but just a few minutes to cut down. In the last 70 years, more than half the world's tropical rainforests have been cut down. There are now fewer trees to absorb carbon dioxide than for thousands of years.

Without trees, less carbon dioxide is removed from the air. The extra carbon dioxide stops heat escaping from Earth into space. As a result, Earth's average temperature rises. This is called **global warming**.

What happens when trees are cut down?

How long would it take you to get soaked in this kind of rain? It is called the rainforest for a reason – it rains a lot! The Amazon basin is home to about 20 per cent of the world's fresh water. The trees suck water from the soil up through their roots. They release **water vapour** into the air through their leaves. The water is **recycled** into Earth's atmosphere, forming clouds. The clouds later release the water as rain.

These floods are in the Beni region of the Bolivian rainforest. What caused the floods? If trees are cut down in rainforest areas, there are fewer tree roots to suck the water out of the soil. Instead the soil becomes **waterlogged**, which causes floods. The water is not recycled into the air. As the water washes down through the soil instead, it pushes the **nutrients** deeper and deeper down. Eventually, it becomes impossible for more trees or other plants to grow on the cleared land.

This woman in Laos is growing crops in a small forest garden.
Her ancestors have lived in forests for hundreds of years. They
have always planted such gardens, without causing any long-term
damage. Several different crops are planted together. Each plant
takes a different kind of **nutrient** from the soil, leaving some behind.
In this way, some nutrients remain.

This giant farm has been carved out of the rainforest. Every year, huge areas of forest in South America, Africa, and Asia are cleared for farmland. Often they are used to grow corn or for cattle farming. Corn crops quickly use up the soil's nutrients. Once the nutrients are gone, the crops can only be grown on the land if farmers use chemical **fertilizers** on the soil. These are expensive and can harm the **environment**.

How does slash-and-burn affect the rainforest?

In most forest areas, the soil does not contain many **nutrients**. If the same crop is grown on it year after year, the soil's nutrients are quickly used up. Because of this, rainforest people such as the Yanomami Indians (pictured) use **slash-and-burn** farming. They cut down the trees and burn the plants to clear land. After a few years of growing crops, they move to a new place. In time, the trees and plants come back, and the soil recovers.

This is a much larger area of land than the Yanomami would
clear. Many poor people come to the rainforest hoping to make
a better life. They clear large areas like this for slash-and-burn
farming. But instead of moving on after a few years, they settle
down. Each year the soil loses more nutrients, and produces less
food. In the end, nothing can grow on the land – not even the trees
that once stood there.

How can music be bad for forests?

Trees are not only cut down to make room for farms. They are also cut down to sell the wood. This is a *koa* tree on the Hawaiian island of Kauai, USA. Its wood is very valuable.

Koa is a **hardwood**, like mahogany, birch, walnut, and maple. Makers of furniture and musical instruments often use hardwoods in their work. *Koa* is especially popular with makers of ukuleles.

Who would have guessed that the tree on the left might become an instrument like the one above? Hardwood instruments such as this ukulele are said to have a better sound than other, cheaper woods.

In poor areas of Asia and South America, hardwood forests are now being cut down in large numbers. This is because hardwoods are so valuable. Today, some types of tree are in danger of disappearing altogether.

How does logging affect forest animals?

Forests are very complicated places. The plants and animals that live in them are all connected to each other. For example, in the rainforest, birds called toucans eat mostly fruit. They then release the fruit seeds in their droppings. Without enough toucans to spread the seeds around, the rainforests would suffer a shortage of fruit trees. Toucans and other animals that eat fruit would go hungry.

How much space is left for the animals that live in this patch of forest? When large areas of forest are cut down, animals have less space to roam in. Finding homes, food, and mates becomes harder. The weaker animals will die out and numbers will shrink.

Rare plants and flowers are also affected. With fewer plants around, insects are less likely to visit them. The plants are not **pollinated**, so they do not **reproduce**. The richness of forest life is lessened.

Why can't this orang-utan find love?

Why might this male orang-utan in Borneo be looking a bit grumpy? Orang-utans once lived in forests throughout Southeast Asia and China. Male orang-utans roamed large areas, looking for a female to mate with. Because they had giant forests to search through, finding a female was easy. Today, finding a mate is much harder.

This photograph shows **logging** in Sabah, Borneo. As forests like this one are cut down, orang-utans have less and less space to live in. This is called **habitat loss**. With only a small area to live in, it is hard for orang-utans to find homes, food, and mates.

Today, orang-utans are an **endangered species**. There are so few of them, there is a risk that they will die out completely.

How does acid rain kill habitats?

This Siberian tiger is lying in the thick, evergreen forests known as **boreal forests**. Boreal forests spread in a circle across North America, northern Europe, and Asia.

Sometimes the **canopy** is so thick that it is dark under the trees, even in daylight. Even so, the forests are home to wolves, bald eagles, bears, Siberian tigers, and many rare plants.

Would you like to get caught in rain that can strip leaves off trees? The Siberian tiger and its fellow creatures do not have a choice. Many boreal forests are affected by acid rain, caused by **pollution** getting into the air. The pollution mixes with the **water vapour** in clouds to form acid. When water vapour falls as rain, the acid comes down, too. It kills trees and other plants, and harms the soil. Sometimes the acid even gets into drinking water. The **habitats** of many rare animals who live in boreal forests are at risk.

What causes forest fires?

This forest in Yellowstone National Park, USA, is recovering from the effects of a fire. Many forest areas need fires. The flames clear away the forest **canopy**, allowing light to flood the forest floor and helping new plants to grow there.

Some trees are triggered into releasing their seeds by fire. Forest plants may have **fire-resistant** seeds, reserve roots that sprout after a fire, or bark that is not affected by fires.

This fire in southern France happened when someone threw away a lit cigarette. Today, some forests are suffering from too many fires. It takes time for plants to grow and animals to return after a fire. If there is another fire too soon, the forest cannot cope.

Campers lighting barbecues and people throwing away lit cigarettes cause hundreds of fires each year. Some fires are even started deliberately by people who want to clear the land for farming.

What happens when logged trees are replaced?

Natural woodland, like this bluebell wood in Hampshire, takes years to develop. It is home to all sorts of different plants and animals.

What happens when woods like this one are cut down? New trees are sometimes planted. Usually they are evergreen trees. Evergreens grow faster than the old trees they have replaced. This means that they can be cut down for timber much sooner.

Imagine how scary it would be finding your way through a dark forest like this one at night! It's not only humans who find forests like this unwelcoming. Compared to the old forest, there are fewer plants and bushes for insects, small animals, and birds to live among. The **habitat** has changed, and the original animals are not **adapted** to life here. Many either leave for new areas, or die out.

These protesters are trying to stop **logging** in Asia. The tiger and orang-utan suits represent two of the many animals that suffer when forests are destroyed. But can our forests be saved?

Small areas of forest are now officially protected. This stops logging, and land being cleared to make farms. Around the world, less than 15 per cent of forests are protected. If all unprotected forests were cut down, it would be disastrous.

What can you do to help save the forests? Each year, forests are cut down to make paper. Using less paper, and **recycling** the paper you do use, is a good way to help save our forests. Re-using old wood, like these doors, also helps. Make sure any new wood you use comes from a **sustainable** source. Most sustainable wood is advertised as such, because then more people are aware that by buying it, they can help save forests.

WHAT DID YOU FIND OUT ABOUT FORESTS?

How do the world's forests keep us all alive?
Hint: the phrase "lungs of the planet" should help you. Also, try going back to pages 6–7 for an explanation.

How many different types of forest can you see in this book? Where in the world are they?
Tip: among them might be rainforests, evergreen **boreal forests**, forests where the trees **shed** their leaves in winter, and mountain forests. Pages 6, 7, 8, 9, 10, 11, 12, 13, and 20 give a few examples.

Make a list of the different things humans get from forests.
Hint: some of them might be immediately obvious, such as wood. Others might be less obvious – how about fresh air and paper, for example?

What are the different threats facing our forests today?
Tip: you don't only have to include direct threats like **logging**. If trees are cut down to make room for cattle farms, maybe the threat is really our demands for meat?

When trees are cut down, do floods become more or less likely? Why is this? Can anything else grow on the flooded soil afterwards?
Hint: look at the photograph on page 9 that shows just a few trees, but a lot of water.

What does cutting down trees do to the soil?
Tip: look at the photographs on pages 9–11 and 13 to find some answers. It's what happens beneath the surface of the soil that is important.

What are the costs of saving our forests?
Hint: try to think of the ways our lives would have to change if we stopped cutting down trees tomorrow. Are there ways in which life would get harder for ordinary people around the world?

What are the benefits of saving our forests?
Tip: there are both obvious and hidden answers to this question. See the chapters throughout the book for answers, but page 5 should provide a helpful summary.

Can you think of any disadvantages to helping to save the forests? Is it possible that there could ever be too many trees on the planet?
Hint: could leaving our trees alone actually damage the **environment**? Do you think you would be able to notice the difference?

What are some things you can do to help save the forests?
Tip: some of them might not be obvious. For example, could what you eat have an effect on the forests? Or perhaps the kind of transport you use? Or even whether you leave the lights on in an empty room? Page 27 might give you some ideas.

Glossary

adapt how a plant or animal changes over time to survive in their habitat

biodiversity range of different living things in an environment. An area's biodiversity includes its animals, plants, fungi, and bacteria.

boreal forest forest in an area with cold, often snowy winters and warm summers. The trees in boreal forests are often evergreens, which keep their leaves all year round.

canopy cover created when the tops of trees grow together, blocking out light

endangered species any type of living thing that is in danger of dying out

environment landscape, soil, weather, plants, and animals that together make one place different from another

equator imaginary line that runs around the centre of Earth. The weather is usually hot and wet around the equator.

fertilizer chemical added to soil to help plants grow. Chemicals washed off the soil and into rivers can affect the plants and animals that live there.

fire-resistant able to survive even if there is a fire

global warming rise in Earth's average temperature

habitat local environment, which is home to particular types of plants

habitat loss destruction of a particular type of habitat. The living things that normally live there have either less space or no space left.

hardwood wood from trees that lose their leaves each year before winter

logging the cutting down of trees for wood, usually to make money

nutrient combination of chemicals that is needed for living things to grow or repair themselves. Plants get some of their nutrients from the soil they grow in.

pollinate help to reproduce, by visits from insects

pollution dirt that harms the environment

recycled when something is used again to make a new product

reproduce make offspring or young. When dogs have puppies they are reproducing.

shed get rid of. Some trees shed their leaves each year before winter.

slash-and-burn farming that involves cutting and burning forests to clear land, then planting crops. Traditionally, the land is only used to grow crops for a few years. The farmers then move on to a new piece of land.

sustainable produced in a way that does not harm the environment

waterlogged full of water

Find out more

Books

Eye Wonder: Rainforest, Helen Sharman (Dorling Kindersley, 2004)

Forest Explorer, Greg Pyers (Raintree, 2004)

Living in the Amazon Rainforest, Anita Ganeri (Raintree, 2008)

Up a Rainforest Tree, Carole Telford and Rod Theodorou
    (Heinemann Library, 2006)

Index